Advice for My Awesome Daughter

Advice for My Awesome Daughter

K. L. Karavatos

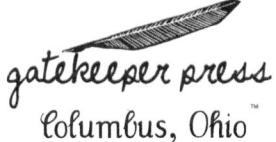

gatekeeper press
Columbus, Ohio

The views and opinions expressed in this book are solely those of the author and do not reflect the views or opinions of Gatekeeper Press. Gatekeeper Press is not to be held responsible for and expressly disclaims responsibility of the content herein.

Advice for My Awesome Daughter

Published by Gatekeeper Press
2167 Stringtown Rd, Suite 109
Columbus, OH 43123-2989
www.GatekeeperPress.com

Copyright © 2021 by K.L. Karavatos
All rights reserved. Neither this book, nor any parts within it may be sold or reproduced in any form or by any electronic or mechanical means, including information storage and retrieval systems, without permission in writing from the author. The only exception is by a reviewer, who may quote short excerpts in a review.

ISBN (hardcover): 9781662916601

For Alexandria Athena Brown

and

Virginia Duston Howell

Foreword

Dear Daughter,

This book contains many of the things I hoped to teach you as you grew up. I can see that you already know many of these insights, and you are already living many these teachings. But just in case you need a little reminder now and then, you can glance at this book.

Please remember, I'm not trying to preach to you. And I realize that, many times, I have failed to follow the advice in this book. But I am evolving (a work in progress), like everyone else. Although I strive to live in harmony with these principles, I am far from perfect.

I have learned so much, and I continue to learn, by being your parent. I feel so blessed to have you as my daughter. My own mother taught me many of the insights I have included in this book. This advice has served me well, by challenging me to be a good human and to forgive myself if I fall short at times. This is advice is given with much love and respect.

You are a wonderful person!

If anyone tries to make you feel inferior, just walk away.

Life is precious, and our time here is short.

HUG the people you love.

The people who deserve to be in your life are the ones who treat you with love, kindness, and respect.

The others are a lesson in what not to become.

Learn the lesson and move on (quickly).

Happiness is often a fleeting state of mind.

Feeling your own wholeness, deep in your soul, is solid and lasting.

Try not to confuse these.

Consult your conscience often and trust your own intuition.

**You are always loved,
more than you know.**

Listen to stillness and marvel at the astounding beauty of nature.

Strive to give voice to your thoughts and feelings.

It's always okay to say no.

Let life touch your soul.

Let in ideas, art, music, literature, love, laughter, kittens, good people, nature . . .

Always remember

(and this is very important):

Your body, <u>your</u> rules!

It's not easy, but strive for the courage to state your opinions.

Don't let fear control you.

You are always braver than you feel.
Everyone feels fear.

Courage is not the absence of fear.

Courage is taking action even when you feel afraid.

Achieve your goals without compromising your values or ideals.

You are always stronger than you think.

Ask "why" and examine authorities. Never blindly follow people or doctrines without analyzing their merits.

Always try to be kind and treat everyone with respect—especially people with less power in society, people who work under you, and people who serve you.

Although it's not always easy,
try to be content.

Remember that
<u>YOU</u> are always enough.

Cherish the good people in your life and let them be in your soul tribe.

True friends are priceless.

Always practice the buddy system in public. *Never* walk alone at night (unless you are walking a very big dog).

Naps are good for you.

Let yourself sleep.

Sometimes your body

and your soul

need to rest.

Although it's romantic to say, "you complete me," strive to be a complete person outside of your relationships.

Try not to define yourself by your relationships or through others.

Try not to look to others to give your life meaning. Decide your own life purposes (even though these may shift and change over time).

Some say that the meaning of life is
... to make your life meaningful.

Try to make a positive difference
in the world.

Try to remember that you cannot *make* another person happy.

People must choose to be happy.

Here is the hard part: Do not try to be an emotional savior to needy people, as they may drain your life force from you, just as a sponge soaks up water.

Some say, "You accept the love you
think you deserve."
I do not know if this is true.
But I do know that
true love is compassionate,
true love is kind,
and true love is gentle.
Try not to accept less.

Do not be too hard on yourself.

Everyone makes mistakes and suffers failures.

If you can correct a mistake, right a wrong, or remedy a failure, do it.

If you cannot, then forgive yourself, apologize to anyone you've hurt, and move forward.

Avoid prejudice! *Never* pre-judge someone based on their appearance, race, gender, culture, accent, background, or other trait. Depth, richness, and meanings in life can often be found in relationships with people who may, at first glance, appear very different from you.

Our minds are powerful.

We often create more of what our minds focus on, whether intentional or not.

Try to focus on the good things in life.

Try to focus on the beauty found in nature.

Allow for the infinite possibilities of the Universe and trust that your life has meaning.

There are miracles around us every moment of our existence.

Take a moment every day to stop, appreciate, and be grateful for the wonder of everything on earth.

Explore new thoughts and ideas with an OPEN mind.

The universe is full of possibilities.

Try not to take yourself too seriously in your daily life.

Allow yourself to be silly.

Life is often more fun that way.

Kindness is the most important practice to humankind.

Always try to be kind and remember that it is never necessary to be unkind.

I love you more than life itself.

As long as I live,

I will always be there for you.

No matter where you are,

you can always come home.

www.ingramcontent.com/pod-product-compliance
Lightning Source LLC
LaVergne TN
LVHW041956060526
838200LV00002B/38